Hope is Your Name

Ayana Maria Dardaine

ISBN 978-1-957956-62-6 (Paperback)
ISBN 978-1-957956-63-3 (Hardcover)
ISBN 978-1-957956-64-0 (Ebook)

Inquiries and Book Orders should be addressed to:

Leavitt Peak Press
17901 Pioneer Blvd Ste L #298, Artesia, California 90701
Phone #: 2092191548
email: info@leavittpeakpress.com

Table of Contents

Foreword

This book is designed to be a source of Inspiration and Hope to Many.

The liberation of Minds towards Greatness
Will continue to expand our Awakening
For a Future that is based on Hope, Love and Peace!

A wise woman once said, "I seek not to proselytize (convert others) but to Be and Live my own Truths."

Some contributions would be freely given to a special environmental project and/ or to any needy family in Trinidad and Tobago or family elsewhere in the world when this book is purchased.

Thank you for Your Hope.

Ayana Maria Dardaine

Hope has a Name...it is You, it is We.

Autobiography

Ayana Maria Dardaine was a firm believer in principle and equity for all. She committed her life through many aspects of her work to fulfill this belief and to ensure that issues and challenges affecting the lives of people could be addressed and rectified. She was passionate about the environment, advocated for education and awareness as well as legislative and policy reform.

She was the Founder and Executive Director of Junior Environmentalists of Trinidad and Tobago (JETT), Community Safety and Disaster Education Committee (CSDEC) and a founding member of many Groups such as Real Voices Youth Group, Trinidad Youth Council (TYC) and many more. She was also a Delegate Country Representative for various events such as UN New York, The 3rd Millennium NGO Forum, Commonwealth Youth Programme, and CSDP Youth Mentorship Programme along with a host of others. Childline Staff Outreach Co-ordinator (2001-2002).

She was a certified Permaculture Designer (Jan 2007) with an Associate Degree in Water Resources Management and Technology (COSTAATT) [2004-2007]. As Chief Editor of Youth Beat Magazine she was focused on development and education of youths both locally and internationally. Ayana was a writer and a poet who loved stories and had one of her poems 'Darkness Is Faded Light' published into the book Taking Flight, The International Library of Poetry (© 2001 Edition).

Her kindness and dedication to the youths will be remembered as a beacon to those who were a part of her life.

Acknowledgments

I would like to give special thanks to God who has made this divinely possible. Thanks to my daughter Ayana for her spiritual inspiration after fasting amidst great distress whilst in Brazil forest (2009). I would also like to thank her two brothers who facilitated the design and layout of this book. It was redesigned to conform to Ayana's original manuscript.

To the designers from KDL and the Leavitt Peak Press publishers, I offer my heartfelt thanks and blessings.

Jean Dardaine (Neé Saunders)
Editor

1

Hope has a Name
We know it as the Divine
Hope has a Name
Known forever in time
Look in the mirror
And say, "My name is…"
Now you know that hope has
a name!

2

Love calls forth
Many answer its call
They are known not by fame
But by their works they are
known
To He/She who matters
This Legion of Energy
Changes the realities of our
time
They are Warriors of Light,
Angels of Light,
Light workers and Peace
Bringers…

They are ordinary people
Working extraordinarily with
the Divine Light.
They are You and We.

3

A Soul's Essence
Is found in every leaf…
Every dew drop…
Every grain of sand…
Every beating heart…
In all life that ever was and
ever will be.

4

Dawn unfolds
Lighting up the heavens
Just as the/your smile
Changes the World!

5

There is hope planted
In the gurgle of a baby
In the pulse of a hand
In the beat of lovers
movements
In the cusp of a palm
All of which blooms
When we open our selves
To their Divine Significance.

6

Dare to hope
To practice its faint glimmer
Allowing it to get brighter
Dare to dream
Of a world made better
Simply because
You dared to hope
And know that
Your hope - Mattered.

7

Simplicity is found
Within a touch,
Divinity-
Within the power of Thought
Translated into Sound
Which becomes the Word.

8

We are all young.
Infants in relation to our
species' place in Time.
Children learn what they live
Ask Yourself:
"What am I teaching my inner
child today?
To help her/him love more?"
Be open to Life's suggestions,
Then Teach!

9

Hope is what drives
All of our tomorrows
And expands
The promise of liberated joy
Each dawn of a new day.

10

Forgive Yourself a thousand
times
For every cruel thought, word
or deed
You ever committed against
Yourself,
Then do the same for those
Who may have done so against
You.

11

We often are quick in our
conclusions
Of world situations and
tribulations.
We sometimes fall prone to
A forgetfulness of past
behaviour and actions
That continue to cause
historical repetitions.
Our time is for the awakening
For the release of eternal
memory
So that our tendency to be
Locked into familiar acts of
passive aggression
We consciously bind
Through Conscientious
planetary action.

12

False representations,
Even with all their grandeur
Don't interest God as much as
Simple renditions of the Heart.
Be conscious of how you pray
Let it be from your Heart and
With the Best Part(s) of You to
offer.

13

Life presents us with
challenges.
They often seem
insurmountable at times.
If we learn to retrain our minds
To see beyond the now
We will understand better how
to cope.
"The problems that I face in
this Now,
Have already been dealt with
in the other."

14

If you could hold in Your Mind
The most powerful notion of
Divine Love ever encountered
How would You use it
To transform Your World?

15

If we only choose to see
The ugliness in the world
We will lose all memory
Of each Beautiful
Emanation of Goodness
Of Light in this space and
place
We call Home... "Terra".

16

As tempting as it is to turn a
blind eye
Against the brutality and
suffering in the world
We must remember
Meditation and prayer must
be followed by action.
Help those who are helping to
change our times
A Helping Hand, Words of
Encouragement and
Meaningful Support.

17

How we treat each other
is reflected by our silent
language
As a species we may yet
understand
How this works,
But it is as real as the Spoken
Word.
What will we do differently?

To respond to the Christ
Consciousness' desire
"Love one another as I have
loved you?"

18

A Deeper Love
Travels through space and time
A Small Act of Love
Travels through space and
time
Love is therefore resonant
Let's choose to spread it
However we can

19

Learning in the Light
Usually is harder
The results...
Our capacity to endure and
love expands
It is "vale a pena" –worth the
challenge

20

Once we learn to transcend
Our fears stemming from our
deepest imaginations
We are given a magnificent gift,
A return to our true selves
By liberating our minds
We free our souls to be.

21

If there was no tomorrow
What would You Do?
Would You Love Differently?
Bring laughter to your vocal
fingertips?
Erupt with Joy among those
You hold most dear?
Would You Relish Your final
sunset?
Drink from the Nectar of the
morning sun?
Bask in the contentment of a
life well-lived?

But we are not asked to worry
about a tomorrow
That may never come.
All we are asked is to know the
Today of This Moment.
So Today...what will You Do
Differently?

22

Walk with me
And let the unfolding of Your
Unconscious Self begin again
How I long for You to See...
See, Yourself as I do.
You are Beautiful.
You radiate such colours
You are My very own Rainbow
A Rainbow of Light,
A Vision of Peace
My Child Consciousness
A Bounty of Perfection
I will wait for You
For You to finally See
The True You
Strong, Resplendent,
A Divine Being in Every Way.

23

People sometimes learn alone
Or so it appears.
There is always a Divine
Collaboration
Of Well-Wishers and Daily
Helpers.
We may not know all of them
Or even remember,
But they number, truly, in
the millions.

24

When we come to realize
That there are no such things
As chance happenings or
accidents.
That every action flows from a
greater divine plan
We can relax...
Take deep breaths
And trust the process...
...for even an incorrect move
is the right one ultimately.

25

A flower is ephemeral
It is delicate and fragile
Yet without the flower
To pollinate life
To feed the birds and the
bees
To bring unadulterated joy
Life as we know it
Would be harsh indeed
Respect and nurture the
Flowers in your life.

26

Life reminds us that
On Life's experiences:
"Consider it Training!"

27

Creation Fire at the heart
Surging winds blow truth
That liberates our souls
Cooling waters of the planet
Flow in peace
Which resonate on the dark
soils of Earth
Yet there is a missing
element
Neither earth nor wind
Nor water nor fire
It is our Will to Love
Our Will to Be
Our Will to Accept
Our role in shaping our
mutual destinies
For we are elemental children
Of Terra
Full of Love, Hope and Divine
Light!

28

If ever You doubt
Your capacity for Greatness,
Take a deep breath and look
directly skywards to the
heavens
Be reminded that:
"I am a product of billions of
years of evolution."
Then get on with the Joy of
Living and Being Great.

29

Where does hope come from?
In the eyes of a stranger
The warmth of a kind touch
The whisper of kindness
The embracing of arms/
The joint union of souls at
work
The kiss of a loved one
The planting of ideas
That nourish and extend

beyond infinite lifetimes.
Now. In the moment.
You are the Hope
We have been waiting for.
You are the One to make Hope
Happen.
One act of Hope at a time.
What Hope will you bring
forth today?

30

Remember that rainy days
Bring with them
Water gives us Life
Nourishing the Earth
Birthing springs
Greening valleys
And when they end for a time
The sun still shines
Both in perpetual Balance
We can learn from
The lessons of rainy days.

31

Who do we trust
To show our Unprotected
Skin?
Who do we trust to reveal
Parts of Our selves uncovered
layer by layer?
Who do we trust?
In those moments when we feel
Most alone?
Trust is learning to Let Love
and Let Go.
Trusting someone begins
When we automatically
Return to a deeper trust
Trusting in our True Self
Trusting in a Higher Power of
Good
Trusting a Universal
Community Benign.

32

You remain "The Best"
The Best Hope
The Best Solution
The Best Beacon Of Happiness
The Best Manifestation
The Best Opportunity for
Growth
Believe it
Become it
For what You have yet to Offer
Is the Best of Who and What
Is to come.

33

We must reconnect
Restore Sacredness
To Our Lives
Nature our true companion
Helps us on our way
If ever we doubt
Take Time
Take Time to Reconnect

Be filled with awe
A Child again
To understand
To appreciate
What it takes to make a
leaf...or a web
To grow 100 feet of towering
canopy
To beat with wings 100 times
per second
Reconnect this moment
Closing your eyes
Stilling your day for a few
minutes
To listen to and reconnect
With your own Wise Soul
Be Happy.
As a Child of the Universe
This Day was also made
For You to Be in it,
My Commitment today is:
"I will reconnect with Nature
And allow my Soul to Heal."

34

Green days by the river
Aquamarine by the sea
Whitened by the snow

Golden with the sunshine
Browned by the Terra Cotta
earth
These and countless other
memories
Spill forth from our global
consciousness
Reminding us gently
Of our Purpose
Our Destiny
Just...Be...
Just...Be...Free...
Just...Be...Free...to Give...
Just...Be...Free...to
Give...And Receive
Blessings and Bounties
To be Shared by All.

35

Ancient Wisdom
Magnetically summons us
We respond
We accede
We respect and reflect
This Ancient Wisdom
Of this Universe
Tuning our Collective Psyches

To Higher Vibrations of
Thought
Leaving lower vibrations
Ascending mentally and
spiritually
As more evolved Beings.

A wise woman once said:
"I seek not to proselytize
(convert others)
But to Be and
Live out My own truths."

36

The world is often harsh
For the Young Initiate
Until She/He realizes
That all acts – even those
Which may hurt
Are still in the end
Wondrous Opportunities for
Soul Growth.

37

Darkness sometimes escapes
through us
And if we are afraid
We may feel devoid of Light
and Hope
It is at these perilous times
WE call forth without shame
our
Divinity...and Divine Helpers
To allow the inner and outer
expansion
Of even the smallest speck of
Light hidden within.

38

Peace is beyond intellectual
conception
It is a Way of Life
When we allow Peace to reside
deep within us
We become Peace Bringers
who unconsciously repeat
daily:

"Peace resides deep within my
Soul and I amplify Peace
Throughout the Universe."
Truly Peace Expands Within
Us.

39

Hope comes from knowing
That there is always a Higher
Divinity at work
There is no such thing as
mundane
All things...
All Beings...
All Acts of Kindness...of
Love...of Hope
Matter.

40

Who determines the depths of
Your Happiness?
As Children of the Universe
WE are Loved.
WE alone are and can

determine
To Be Happy.
Believe in God/Goddess You
Know.
Remember Your degree of
Happiness
Adds Infinite Joy to this World
And to the Cosmos.

41

Respect the Balance
Our oceans and life within
Rivers, streams, hills, forests,
valleys
The Beings within them
Respect the Balance
We have taken so much
And given so little
Now our Planet calls on Us
To diminish our waste-
fulness
Reduce our materialistic
patterns
Clean the junk yards of our
Collective Minds,
Turning them into nurturing
Watersheds.

Saving our Energy to learn
Alternative Ways of Being We
have been summoned To an
Urgent Call
Simply to...
Respect The Balance.

42

What does it mean to live?
Truly...go beyond mere
existing?
We are tiny bits of charcoal
Pressurized over Time
Becoming Diamonds in the
Rough
It is our Character
Our sensing of Self
Our capacity to Seek, Seed,
and Explore New Horizons
To Heal and Be Healed
To Love and Let Love
That makes the pressurization
process worthwhile.
And remove us from a lack-
luster finish.

43

What can be said?
Of the Love that encourages us
To nurture and heal our Planet
It is the same Love that is
unlocked
When seeding the earth
It is the same Love
That flourishes with a
Bountiful Harvest
It is the Love of Feeling
The Love of Doing
For this Love goes Beyond
Any disconnect
And helps restore us
To a State of Grace
All Beings
Intertwined,
Interrelated
Interdependent...as
One very Diverse Whole.

44

We might think
That we are beyond Hope since
Our indiscretions enhance our
personal shame
We may even experience
impotence
To act even on our own behalf
It is during these times of
self-absorbing thought
We should remember
Our Divine Ancestry
Gives us the Divine Power
To Transform
All ungainly thought patterns
It is a Divine Gift as Children
of the Universe
To Become
To Evolve
To Light Up the World
As We were always meant to
Do
Now and In the Ever.

45

When we have the courage to
face our own death
It is at that moment of Divine
Choice and Acceptance
That we encounter
Truly
Our Divine Immortality.

46

Saving the world
Begins with a thought
Trust one that resonates within
your universe
That connects with others
Let that one thought be filled
with,
Joy, Hope, Love & Goodness,
Hold it fixedly in Your Mind.
Then Let Go.
Apply some of its truths
And Allow the process of
Positive Change

Unfold the miracles within
and without.

47

Who can accurately predict
the future?
We can.
God/Goddess/The Great
Spirit/Universal Mind
Gave each and everyone of us
The Divine Power
To mold,
To craft
Our realities through the
Divinity's Will...
If we centre our predictions
on
a World of Hope
We Being thinking that way...
We can then put into
practice...
The Hope needed to Awaken
others...
To become same.

48

Justice without compassion
Is no justice at all
How will we treat with those
who have gravely erred?
Divine Karma/Justice will
unfold as it should
Yet still we are called upon
To temper reparation with
conciliation
For Peace to Reign Supreme.

49

When seeking Truth,
Give Yourself Over
Let go to the Universal Mind
And allow Your Divine
Helpers
To Guide You to the
Truth You Seek.
You will realize then
That it has always and will
ever be...
Within You.

50

We keep waiting for change to
happen
We see people homeless
Children begging in the street
And we think someone (else)
will help them.
The truth is someone else
usually does.
Now You are called upon
To Be that Someone Else too
Remember small acts
Lead to Great Things.

51

Children bring us Hope,
They remind us
We were all - no matter where
we are in Life
Or what we have done in the
past or recent present
All of us were Born Perfect
In Every Way,

That's how the Universe
Through the Gift of Children
Remind us we can change for
the Better!

52

Our Planet reminds us
Of God's/Goddess'
magnificent handiwork.
I am always in awe
At the profound Beauty of it all.
Take time to raise Your hands
Look up at the New Dawn
Or estrellas (stars) in the Sky.
There is Hope in the Heavens too.

53

Even the smallest speck of
Light
Shines brilliantly in the
Darkness.

54

To know God/Goddess/Great
Spirit/Universal Mind
Is to know Love
To know Love
Is to Practice it Fully.

55

Wisdom comes from knowing
That there is Inherent Joy
In meeting even one's Own
Death
For the Greater Good of All
Under Heaven and Above Earth.

56

For our lives to Change
It takes Courage
It takes Love
It takes Hope
It takes Movement
What will you do in Your Life
Today
To Change Your World?

57

Moving away from deception
Is easier than we think
It starts by making a
conscientious decision
Daily, moment by moment
That I: "Choose to be true to
myself...and honest
With those whom I come
across."
Then let the Power of Your
Own Will to Change
Do the Rest.

58

Many of us have been
Victims of the worse kind of
atrocities...
Rape, incest, emotional
vampirism;
We've been beaten, used,
abused, kicked, cuffed
And for some often been
broken.
What Hope is there for any
Soul so hurt?
And so badly damaged?
The First Flow is Clearance
The clearing out of the inner
guilt of any wrong committed
against us.
It helps to even say (as one
Shaman declared):
"I release you...I release me."
To recapture the part of Your
Stolen Soul
For Soul theft is real under
trauma.
The Second Flow allows
Divine Helpers to Heal
The Inner You, The Inner

Child Within.
With a deep promise to Your
Self
To be Patient during the
Healing Process
To honour and expand the Best
of the True You
To Recapture Loving the
Perfect Being That is You.
There is Hope. Time Heals All.

59

There are moments when Even
the most determined of us
Fall back on old habits or
patterns of decay.
Isn't it good to know
Since we've been there before
We already know the way out?

60

Imagine a world Free from
war, Free of hardship and the
bonds of fear and hate.

Imagine a world Free from
want.
Imagine, Imagine, Imagine it.
Then,
Allow Your Mind
To Let such a world happen
and Come into Being.

61

I've met Children who
Scarred by their experience of war
So young, so young
Find it near impossible to
believe
In a World of Peace
I believe we owe it
To those Children
That the dream of a Peaceful
World
Becomes their Reality.

62

If all leaders have followers
And all followers are leaders
Then all Leaders at some point
in their Lives
Be Followers too!
Find, express and shine the
Inner Leader in You.

Are found everywhere in our
world story
The inspired daily worker, the
prolific teacher,
The powerful group influencer
All used one same tool.
The power of mental invention
And practiced their Vision
To make a more Caring and
Meaningful World Happen.
Practice Your Mental Influence
To Bring Hope into a New
World.

63

People who Change History
For the Better
Often don't consciously know
They're Doing it,
But they are consciously
determined to try
In their own way
To make their contribution to
the Collective Goodwill
Often without a road map.
Sometimes unsure of impact or
destination.
These Great Pioneers,
Men, Women and Children of
Caliber

64

What is a Crisis...
But a Golden Opportunity
To work with Divine
Influence?
To transform, learn and
encounter?
The Power of Meditation
The Power of Prayer
The Power of God/Goddess
Divine
To work within humans and
other species
Towards Divine Solutions.

65

When we learn to See
The Soul Consciousness
Of every Being.
We will no longer
Judge them by our fear of the
Unknown or
Our unconscious prejudices.
For all Souls stem from the
Same Source
One Mass of Consciousness...
A Collective Whole.
"Today I choose to Respect
The Divinity and Soul
Consciousness of All."

66

Soul laughter works Wonders
When we are faced with
Difficult spasmodic situations
It lessens their temporal gravity
Which weighs down the intellect
And Frees us up to Become

Divine conduits
Capable of engaging and
embracing Daily Miracles.

67

To Awaken Others...
Bring Hope.
Your Life
Is Your Message of Hope.

68

Change comes about...
A pen stroke...
The pounding of feet...
The union of Minds
The Will to Be More
Do remember this:
Inspired Thought is followed
by
Inspired Action
It requires us to
Think Big
Even if we act small

For many small acts
Lead to Great Things
Have Faith in Yourself
You are not alone
In Your Good Intent
Become Aware, Alive and
Awake
And Bring Hope
By Your Life's Work.

69

When You Think of the Future
Be Happy
Be Joyous
Fill Your Spirit with Laughter
Even as You Center Your Self
with Peace
Let Love radiate in Your Mind
For the Future
Is Yet to Become
It awaits Your Uplifted
Thinking
For a Positive Outcome.

70

We declare
Our Divine Right to dance in
the Sun.
Celebrate Our Diversity
Honour Our Spirituality
Salvage Our Beloved Planet's
Dignity
Free the Hungry minds and the
Disadvantaged,
This we Declare...
Today and Always
Our Divine Right,
Our Divine Responsibility
To restore Balance, Grace and
expand Divine Beauty,
This we joyously declare.
Coming together
To discuss our planet's future
Goes beyond fairytale whispers
Or silky threads of illusion.
It is happening now.
And You, My Friend,
With Your Own Special
Talents
And Divine Light
Will be called upon

To add your Unique Energies
To See Us...
As one Collective...
Through.

72

71

For many moons
We have endured,
Now we are at the crossroads.
All that we have and are
Is borne from a plundered earth
Watering our machines.
Even the food consumed
The Love we make.
What will we do this Very Day?
To go beyond Endurance,
To live symbiotically,
For all sakes and all
generations.
It begins with a Committed
Will,
Live and Respect
That which keeps us Alive.
Each act of determined Will to
Love Matters.

Our world is on the brink
ON the brink of Hope
On the brink of Change
On the brink of an armless
revolution
Though many arms are jointly
at work
How was it possible?
Every Believer brings with
her/him
The Breath of Hope,
Yours added to Mine added to
His, to Hers to Theirs...
Becomes a Wind,
A Wind of Collective Changes
For a Far Better World,
More Peaceful,
A More Caring Place and
Space in Time.

73

Does love cancel out hate?
Do you believe that it does?
Stop for a minute
And Think of a World
Completely Filled with Love
What did it look like?
How did it feel?
Your thought of Love at that moment
Canceled out hate the same moment
Because it ceased to exist in your own thoughts
Even for that brief moment
Does Love cancel out hate?
Yes.
It does.

It is the
Thought of Love,
Transfusing,
Transforming
Our realities.
Use the Power
Held within the Divine Power
That is You
To cancel Hate.
One Moment,
But a Billion Thoughts
At a Time

74

And the final act
Of the Peace Revolution is...
...
Changed!

3 de março de 2009
Ayana-maria

3 Years

12 Years

In Loving Memory of

Ayana Maria Dardaine
19th January, 1978 - 17th March, 2012.
"Some of them left a name behind them,
so that their praises are still sung."
Sirach 44:8

May the smile you radiate heal hearts, Love Always.
From: Your Loving Mum, Dad, Brothers,
Aunts, Uncles, Cousins, Friends and Well Wishers.

Photo - 29 Years
Heavenly rest in 2012 (34 Years)

About the Author

Ayana Maria Dardaine was a firm believer in principle and equity for all. She committed her life through many aspects of her work to fulfill this belief and to ensure that issues and challenges affecting the lives of people could be addressed and rectified. She was passionate about the environment, advocated for education and awareness as well as legislative and policy reform.

She was the Founder and Executive Director of Junior Environmentalists of Trinidad and Tobago (JETT), Community Safety and Disaster Education Committee (CSDEC) and a founding member of many Groups such as Real Voices Youth Group, Trinidad Youth Council (TYC) and many more. She was also a Delegate Country Representative for various events such as UN New York, The 3rd Millennium NGO Forum, Commonwealth Youth Programme, and CSDP Youth Mentorship Programme along with a host of others. Childline Staff Outreach Co-ordinator (2001-2002)

She was Chief Editor of Youth Beat Magazine and focused on development and education of youths both locally and internationally. Ayana was a writer and a poet who loved stories and had one of her poems 'Darkness Is Faded Light' published into the book Taking Flight, The International Library of Poetry (© 2001 Edition).

Her kindness and dedication to the youths will be remembered as a beacon to those who were a part of her life.

www.ingramcontent.com/pod-product-compliance
Lightning Source LLC
Chambersburg PA
CBHW051602120626
46551CB00013B/1638